# Brother Sun,
# Sister Moon

# Brother Sun, Sister Moon

## The Story of St Francis

Margaret Mayo

*illustrated by*
Peter Malone

Orion
Children's Books

For my husband, Peter

M M

To Phoebe and Imogen

P M

First published in Great Britain in 1999
by Orion Children's Books
a division of the Orion Publishing Group Ltd
Orion House, 5 Upper St Martin's Lane, London WC2H 9EA

A catalogue record for this book is available from the British Library

Designed by Louise Millar

Printed in Italy

# Contents

# The Glorious Little
# Poor Man of Assisi

All over the world, people still talk about the great man, Saint Francis, who was born more than eight hundred years ago in the Italian city of Assisi. The man who came from a wealthy family, yet chose to be poor.

He was the son of a cloth merchant, and at the time of his birth, his father was in the south of France. On returning home, he affectionately named his new son "the Frenchman" – Francesco (Francis in English).

Francis grew up in the age of the Crusades, and
his dream was that one day he would win fame as a
brave knight in shining armour. He sometimes
worked with his father, selling woollen cloth at local
markets, but mostly he led a carefree life. His parents
gave him everything he wanted, and he spent money
extravagantly on himself and his friends. He liked to
wear brightly coloured, expensive clothes, and he
enjoyed jokes and surprises.

Once he had a cloak made of a patchwork of rich fabric and old rags. It was the talk of the city!

When he met with his friends, they feasted on rich food and wine. They watched jugglers and acrobats, or listened to singers and musicians – and Francis, who loved to sing, would often join in.

When he was twenty, war broke out between the cities of Assisi and Perugia. Dressed in shining armour and mounted on a splendid horse, Francis rode off, eager for victory and glory. But the battle was short. Assisi was defeated and Francis captured. He spent a year in a cold, dirty prison. There he fell ill and was only released when his father paid a ransom.

After a long illness, Francis returned to his old life of luxury and pleasure. Illness and prison had changed him though, so that now he would sometimes walk alone in the hills, thinking and praying.

Out riding in the country one day, Francis saw a man who had leprosy. Francis was about to toss a few coins and ride by when he was overcome by a feeling of deep pity. He jumped to the ground, placed the coins in the leper's hand, and then kissed the hand. From that time on, he regularly visited the little lepers' house outside Assisi, bringing gifts of food and clothes.

On another day, not long after, Francis was in the ruined church of San Damiano, outside Assisi.

While he was praying, he heard a voice say, "Francis, my church is falling down. Repair it for me."

Francis was happy. He was sure God had spoken to him. He hurried home, loaded a few bales of his father's woollen cloth on a horse and rode to the nearby town of Foligno. Then he sold the cloth, and the horse as well.

Francis walked back to San Damiano, found the priest and offered him a bag of money. The priest refused to accept it because the money really belonged to Francis's father. Thoroughly upset and disappointed, Francis tossed the bag on to a window ledge and left.

His father was furious when he heard what his son had done and in the end Francis left home and lived rough out in the open, sleeping in caves and begging for food. Finally his father accused him of stealing and Francis was ordered to appear before the court of the Bishop of Assisi.

Francis arrived at the court with the bag of money in his hand. He had gone back to San Damiano and found it still on the window ledge. Quietly he placed the bag at his father's feet and then he really surprised everyone. He took off all his clothes and placed them beside the bag.

"I have returned everything," said Francis. "And now I have only one Father who is in heaven."

His father said nothing, and sadly was never to speak to Francis again. The Bishop, however, draped his cloak around Francis and sent a servant to find some old clothes for him to wear.

When Francis left the Bishop's palace, he knew

he was beginning a new life. He would be a knight after all, serving Jesus, the King. There was snow on the ground but as he walked through the woods outside Assisi, he was so happy, he sang one of his favourite songs.

For the next two years, besides caring for lepers, Francis was busy repairing three ruined churches. He worked with his own hands, begging for stones and anything else he needed. He lived alone and prayed. He studied the sun, moon and stars, the wind and rain, the trees and flowers. He had a special affection for all birds and animals, fish and insects. He called them his brothers and sisters.

One of his favourite birds was the hooded lark. "Sister Lark, you are a humble bird," he said. "Your feathers are not bright. They are the colour of the earth. But, Sister Lark, when you fly, you sing the sweetest and loveliest of songs."

In church one day, Francis heard a priest read from the Bible some words Jesus had said: *Go and tell everyone the good news about God. Go two by two. Don't take anything with you. No money. No extra clothes or food. There is no need to wear shoes or carry a staff.*

Francis knew immediately that this was how he must live. It was 24th February, 1208, and he was twenty-six years old. From then on Francis walked barefoot and wore a long rough tunic, tied round the waist with a rope. He started visiting the market place in Assisi and stood there talking about God. Gradually, people stopped and listened.

Within a few weeks, three men asked if they could join him and he agreed. But first they had to sell everything they had and give their money to the poor. One of them, Bernard, was very rich indeed.

They all had to wear the same simple clothes as Francis. They had to work with their hands to earn any food or clothes they needed, otherwise they had to beg. At night they slept in huts made of woven branches, in caves or under the sky.

They spent many hours praying, and two by two they visited other towns and villages nearby and told people about God's love and forgiveness.

After a year, Francis had eleven companions. Together they wrote down a few rules describing how they should live. Then they walked to Rome, where they saw the Pope, and he gave his approval of their way of life.

Francis called the group *Friars Minor*, which
means lesser brothers. He did not want them to have
a grand, important-sounding name. The number of
companions, or brothers, grew rapidly, and soon they
were travelling further and further – to Spain, Ger-
many and North Africa. On one occasion, Francis
himself travelled to Egypt where some Crusaders
were fighting but he was horrified by the killing and
suffering of war.

In 1212, an eighteen-year-old girl, Lady Clare, who was a nobleman's daughter, left her home in Assisi. She too wanted to live a life of prayer and poverty, and Francis welcomed her. She was given a tunic like his to wear and her long hair was cut off. Then she went to live in a house with a garden around it, close by the church of San Damiano which Francis had repaired.

Before long other women joined her. In those days women could not travel freely or speak in public places as Francis did, so they led a quiet life, praying for hours and gardening. Francis called Clare and the other women 'the Poor Ladies', and today there are still women who live like them. They are known as *Poor Clares*.

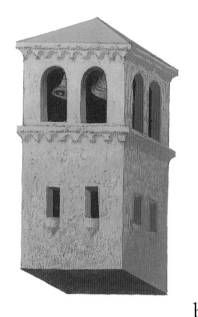

Eventually, Francis was
so well loved that when he
came to a town or village
the church bells were rung,
children clapped and waved
branches in the air, and people ran
towards him and tried to touch him.

His greeting was always: *God give you peace.*
And then he spoke simply and clearly using words
that everyone would understand.

Even when he was famous, and there were
hundreds of brothers, he was still the same Francis
in his rough patched tunic. The man who loved
peace, who spent many hours in prayer and called
himself the champion of Lady Poverty. The man who
liked to joke and sing and tease his friends.

In his last years, Francis was often ill. He suffered great pain and gradually became blind. He died in 1226, when he was not quite forty-five years old.

It is said that on the day Francis died a flight of larks gathered above the roof of the place where he lay, and flying low, they wheeled in a great circle, singing sweetly as they flew.

# How Francis Tamed
# a Ferocious Wolf

Once a large and most ferocious wolf roamed the hills about the town of Gubbio in Italy. The wolf was ravenously hungry and killed and ate not just animals, but humans too.

Everyone was terrified of him, and because he often came right up to the town wall, no one felt safe: the children playing in the fields, the grape pickers in the vineyard, the peasant in the olive grove, not even the woodcutter in the forest.

A time came when no one would venture out into the country unless fully armed, as if off to war. But the wolf was cunning and quick, and even with weapons, it was impossible to escape his sharp teeth and cruel jaws.

All people could talk about was the wolf. Even at night they couldn't forget him because he howled, loud and long, until it wasn't just the children who pulled the bedclothes over their ears.

Then Francis and a brother came to Gubbio. When he heard about the wolf, Francis was sad and deep-down sorry for the frightened people. "I must go and talk to Brother Wolf," he said.

That upset everyone. "No, no, no!" they said. "Don't go outside the gates, Brother Francis! The wolf is sure to kill you!"

"Don't be afraid. The Maker of All Things will take care of me," said Francis. And without even picking up a stick to defend himself, he strode off.

The brother hurried after him, trying to keep up, and a few brave young peasants followed behind. But when the young men found themselves outside the town, their feet grew heavy and they lagged behind. They were scared.

Francis turned round. "Wait here," he said. "I'll go on and find the wolf." Off he strode again, with the brother still hurrying after, trying his best to keep up!

Meanwhile, back in Gubbio, the town walls, trees and roofs were crowded with men, women and children, eyes big and round, mouths wide open, watching and wondering . . . what would happen next?

And then . . . there was a flurry of grey fur, a

flash of white teeth and the wolf came running, bounding, almost flying down the hillside.

Francis stood motionless. He raised his hand and made the sign of the cross. For a moment the wolf hesitated, checked himself, then closed his cruel jaws and slowed down until he was walking.

Francis called, "Come, Brother Wolf! And don't hurt me or anyone else. It's in the name of Christ that I'm telling you this."

Then something amazing happened. The large and most ferocious wolf walked up to Francis, bowed his head and stretched out on the ground, burying his nose between his paws.

'Brother Wolf . . . Oh, Brother Wolf . . ." sighed Francis. "You have done so many wicked things. I know you were hungry, but you killed again and again. Now everyone hates you and wants to get rid of you. But I want to make peace between you and them."

At this the wolf lifted his head and pricked up his ears. "First, Brother Wolf," Francis continued, "you must show me that you are sorry for what you have done." The wolf nodded his head. He moved his ears up and down and thumped his tail.

"Good," said Francis. "Now I promise that the people of Gubbio will feed you generously every day, for as long as you live, if you promise never again to hurt any living creature, animal or human. Will you agree to this?"

The wolf nodded his head. Francis held out his right hand, and the wolf raised his right paw, and they shook hand and paw, solemnly, seriously.

"Come with me into the town," said Francis. He smiled. "No need to be frightened, Brother Wolf!"

Off he strode, with the wolf trotting by his side like a pet lamb, and the brother still following behind trying his best to keep up!

And in Gubbio? There was big excitement. By the time Francis and the wolf reached the market place it was full of people, craning their necks, jumping up and down, all wanting to see for themselves Francis and the wolf.

"Peace, dear people of Gubbio!" said Francis, and immediately there was a hush. "Good news! Brother Wolf wants to tell you he is truly, deeply sorry for the wicked things he has done. And more good news! He has promised not to hurt any living creature ever again, if you will promise to feed him generously every day. I know I'm asking a big, big favour, but will you forgive him? Will you treat him kindly and feed him?"

A roar of voices greeted him. "We promise!" they shouted. "Brother Francis, we promise!"

"Brother Wolf," said Francis, "show everyone that you are truly, deeply sorry and make your promise again, in front of them."

And that large and most ferocious wolf stretched out on the ground, nodded his head, moved his ears up and down and thumped his tail, as if to say 'sorry'.

Francis held out his right hand, and the wolf raised his right paw, and again they shook hand and paw.

How happy everyone was! Another roar of shouts rose up and up, until it seemed to reach the sky. C hildren jigged and danced, clapping wildly. Men waved their arms in the air. Women hugged their babies.

"Thank you, Brother Francis," they shouted.
"Thanks and praise to our Father in Heaven for
sending you to us!"

A few days later, Francis and the brother left Gubbio.
There were other towns and villages they had to visit.

But the wolf and the people of Gubbio kept their
peace promise. The wolf hurt no one and no one hurt
him. He walked freely from door to door like a
friendly pet. He was always welcomed and fed
generously. And perhaps most surprising of all, not a

single dog barked or growled when he walked by.

When at last the wolf grew old and died, everyone was sad, especially the children. For they had grown to love Brother Wolf.

The years passed, but they never forgot gentle Francis and how he tamed a ferocious wolf. They told the story again and again to their children, to their grandchildren, to their great grandchildren . . . and that wonderful, remarkable story has lived on, even to this day.

# Francis Talks to the Birds

Early one morning Francis and some brothers set off on a journey through the Italian countryside. It was a beautiful day, and they left the roads and followed winding paths – past sprouting vines, through green and silver olive groves, skirting fields of freshly sprung corn.

They came to a grassy meadow, with a few
scattered bushes and a little wood beside it, and there
were birds everywhere. They covered the grass, filled
the trees and bent down the bushes. There were birds
of every kind – larks and doves, crows, jackdaws and
swallows and many more besides. It almost seemed
as if they were waiting for someone.

When Francis saw them, he didn't stop and stare.
He loved birds and was so delighted that he ran
eagerly towards them. The birds did not fly off. They
didn't flutter a feather. They were not scared.

The watching brothers were astonished, and when Francis stopped and looked around, so was he!

"Little Sisters," he said. "Peace . . ." And the birds quietly tilted their heads towards him, as if they were listening. "My dear little Sisters, you have been given so much. Think about it! You are marvellously made. You've got feathers to keep you warm, wings so you can fly wherever you wish. As for food, it's all around and free. You don't have to dig the ground and plant seeds. So for all this, my Sisters, you should always and in every place sing songs of praise to your Maker."

The birds opened their beaks and flapped their wings, all the time gazing intently at Francis.

Quietly, thoughtfully, Francis walked among the birds, touching their heads, stroking their wings. Many of those on the trees flew towards him, some landing by his feet, and others fluttering about him or coming to rest on his shoulders or outstretched arms.

At last Francis raised a hand and made the sign of the cross. "Fly away little Sisters," he said. "But don't forget, wherever you are, sing songs of praise!"

All the birds spread their wings, and flew up, higher and higher, a glorious whirling mass of wings and feathers.

Francis walked back to the brothers who had been watching. "This is the first time I've ever talked to our sisters the birds," he said. "But it won't be the last. I think they understood what I said."

The brothers nodded their heads. They had to agree.

# The Ox, the Ass and
# the Child of Bethlehem
## A Christmas Story

Francis was always doing the unexpected. He was full of surprises, and one of his loveliest, happiest surprises happened at Christmas time.

About three years before he died, Francis and a few brothers were living in some caves on a mountainside, close by the small town of Greccio. It was nearly Christmas, his favourite festival. He called it the Feast of Feasts.

Francis was thinking about the birth of Jesus.
"I wish I could make it real," he thought. "So that
everyone could see for themselves the poor, humble
place where the Child of Bethlehem, Christ the
King, was born. Not in a palace, but in a stable." Sud-
denly his eyes lit up. He knew what he was
going to do . . .

Francis had been ill and was often in great
pain, so he found John, a brother who was a very
close friend. "I need your help," said Francis. "For
something special. On Christmas Eve, this is what
you must do . . ." Then Francis explained his plan.
"But keep it secret. It's to be a surprise."

On Christmas Eve John called at the house of an old peasant. "May I borrow your ox?" he asked. "Brother Francis needs it tonight, for something special."

"You can borrow anything for Brother Francis," said the old man, who like many people loved Francis dearly.

"May I borrow your ass too? And some hay and the manger?" said John.

"Of course," said the old man. "But what for? Tonight of all nights! It's Christmas Eve!"

John raised a finger to his lips. "It's a secret. A big surprise," he whispered. "Come to Midnight Mass at the church in the woods, and you will see!"

So the animals' manger, stuffed full of hay, was loaded on to the back of a little ass, and away went John, driving the ass and a hefty ox before him.

All day the news flew round the small town. A big surprise . . . tonight . . . Midnight Mass at the church in the woods . . . Francis will be there.

Late that evening, doors were flung open and banged shut. Young and old came skipping and walking, shuffling and hobbling out of their houses, everyone holding high a candle or flaming torch to light up the dark night.

Laughing and singing, they wound their way through the woods. One by one, they entered the church, and then "Ohhh!" they gasped. What a surprise!

There, in the church, was a manger full of hay and standing beside it were the hefty ox and the little ass. Close by was Francis, thin and frail, in his brown patched robe – but smiling as he gazed lovingly at the manger, as if the baby Jesus lay there.

The service began. The priest celebrated mass over the manger. Then Francis sang in his beautiful, clear voice the words from the Gospel describing the birth of Jesus. When he had finished, he spoke about the Child of Bethlehem, Christ the King.

"He was not born in a palace, but in a stable," said Francis. "Look and always remember. He was poor, and he was humble."

To the people in the church, it seemed then as if there *was* a baby lying in the hay, in the simple, roughly made manger, just as there had been at Bethlehem, long ago.

And so the night of celebration ended, with young and old walking back through the woods, full of wonder and joy and peace.

Francis's lovely, happy surprise has been copied in different ways ever since. Today, throughout the world, nativity scenes are set up at Christmas to make more real to everyone the poor and humble birth of Jesus, the Child of Bethlehem.

# Some Little Tales

# The Trapped Hare

One day, when walking in a wood, one of the brothers found a little hare caught in a trap. He bent down and carefully set it free. But the frightened hare just lay there and wouldn't move, so the brother picked it up and brought it to Francis.

"Dear Brother Hare," murmured Francis, wrapping his arms around the frightened little hare and holding it tenderly. "I thought you were a clever little brother. But – one jump – and there you were in a trap. How did you let yourself be tricked like that?"

48

Francis stroked his soft fur and the little hare snuggled up to him. "Feeling better now?" he asked. "Really? Well then, off you go and live wild and free, back in the woods. But don't get tricked! Look out for traps!"

Very gently he put the little hare down on the ground. But – one jump – and it was back in his arms. Again he put it down, and again it jumped back. A *third* time he put it down, and a *third* time it jumped back.

"I guess you won't leave until I'm out of sight," said Francis. "Best ask the good brother who found you to take you back to the woods . . ."

And that was exactly what the brother did. Then, at last, the little hare jumped off, ready and happy, to live once more wild and free.

# The Noisy Swallows

Early one evening a big crowd gathered in a certain market square. Francis had come to their town, and they all wanted to see him and hear what he had to say.

Now Francis was not very tall so, in order that everyone could see him, he climbed to the top of a flight of steps. He held up his hand and the crowd fell silent.

"My Brothers and Sisters, God give you peace," he began. Then he stopped. He couldn't hear a word he was saying. Nor could anyone else.

In the cool of the evening a flock of swallows had gathered in the market square. Some were swooping, circling and calling, while others were twittering non-stop as they busied about, to and fro, building their nests. What a noise!

Francis looked up and stared at those swallows. "My Sisters! Be quiet up there!" he called out. "It's my turn now! You've had your say!"

Instantly the swallows that were swooping and circling flew down and landed on the roofs, while the others stopped twittering and nest-building. Every swallow was absolutely still, absolutely silent.

So Francis began to talk about God and how people should live. He used simple words, as he always did, and just listening to him made everyone feel happy.

When he had finished, all the people whispered to one another, "Brother Francis must be a saint. Only a saint could silence those noisy swallows."

As he left, they pressed close up to him and reached out to touch that special, good and lovable man – Brother Francis.

# The Playful Fish

One day Francis was crossing a lake in a boat when a fisherman caught a rather large fish.

"For you, Brother Francis! A gift!" said the fisherman, handing him the still very much alive, tail-flapping fish.

Francis was delighted. He thanked the fisherman for his generosity and took firm hold of the slippery, still very much alive, tail-flapping fish.

"Brother Fish," said Francis. And there was a glint in his eye. "Beautiful Brother Fish, don't worry. I'm not going to eat you. No, you belong in the water."

Francis leant over the side of the boat, and he dropped the fish back into the lake.

Then Francis, as he often did, began to pray. And while he prayed, the fish leapt out of the water and dived in again. Out and in, it playfully followed the boat. On and on.

When Francis finished praying, he opened his eyes. "Still here, Brother Fish?" he said. "Didn't you know it was time to go home?"

So with one final dive, down and down, the playful fish was gone.

# The Cicada's Song

An old fig tree grew near a small hut where Francis sometimes slept, and every day, about the same time, a cicada would hop on to one of the branches and chirp a lively song.

One day Francis held out his hand and said, "Sister Cicada, come." And the cicada hopped on to his hand. "Now Sister Cicada, sing! Praise your Maker with a happy song!"

The cicada began to chirp, and Francis, who loved to sing, joined in. The two of them sang a duet. When they had both sung quite long enough, Francis smiled and nodded his head, and the cicada hopped off his hand and back on to the fig tree.

Each day after that, when the cicada put in an appearance on the fig tree, Francis was waiting. The cicada hopped on to his hand, and they sang their duet.

The singing became a big attraction and so much fun that all the brothers came to watch. But on the seventh day, Francis said, "Sister Cicada, I really must give you permission to get on with your own life. You've given us so much happiness. But enough is enough! So – goodbye, little Sister! Goodbye!"

And the cicada hopped off and was never seen again on that old fig tree.

# The Friendly Falcon

In the last few years of his life, Francis suffered a great deal of pain and was often tired and ill. But he still liked to visit quiet, remote places, where he could think and pray undisturbed.

Once when he was living alone in a little hut, up in the hills, he made friends with a falcon who was building a nest there. They seemed to understand each other. Early most mornings Francis woke while it was dark and began to pray, and as he prayed, the falcon beat his wings.

Sometimes – just sometimes – Francis overslept. Then the falcon would call out, very loudly, and wake him. This amused Francis.

"Now I have Brother Falcon to wake me," he said, "I've got no excuse if I get up late, except downright laziness!"

Then something strange happened. One night Francis was ill. He was in so much pain, he sighed and groaned, and next morning he overslept. But the falcon didn't make his waking call at the usual time, while it was dark. He waited till the sun had risen, and then called to Francis.

" My kind-hearted friend," said Francis. "You thought I needed extra sleep and rest, didn't you?"

The falcon beat his wings.

"Yes, I know," said Francis. "It's time to pray!"

# Brother Sun . . . Sister Moon

No one could guess that this joyful poem *The Canticle of Brother Sun* was written by Francis during his final illness, in the year before he died. Although he was suffering intense pain, he also composed a melody for the words and urged the brothers to sing the song whenever they could.

# Brother Sun . . . Sister Moon

All praise to you, most high, all powerful, all good Lord.
To you alone, all praise belongs.
Praise to you, through everything you have made . . .

All praise, my Lord, through Sister Moon and the Stars,
   set in the sky, so wonderful and bright.

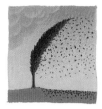

All praise, my Lord, through Brothers Wind and Air,
    and all the weathers, cloudy, calm or stormy,
      by which you nourish all you have made.

All praise, my Lord, through Sister Water,
    so precious, useful, humble and pure.

All praise, my Lord, through Brother Fire,

who lights up the night.

How joyful he is! How beautiful and strong!

All praise, my Lord, through Sister Earth,

our mother who feeds us

and gives us fruits and herbs and coloured flowers.

Praise and bless my Lord.
Thank him and serve him
With great humility.

# Saint Francis

## 1181-1226

At the time of his death, Saint Francis was so loved and admired that it was soon decided that the story of his remarkable life should be written down. Within three years, Brother Thomas of Celano had completed just such a book. Several other accounts followed not long after, and some of Saint Francis's own writings were also carefully preserved. Perhaps the most famous book about him, *The Little Flowers*, or *Fioretti*, is quite different. It was written about 1330 and was based on stories which had been passed down by word of mouth. The story of the wolf of Gubbio is to be found in this collection.

In 1228 Pope Gregory IX proclaimed Francis a saint, and ordered the building of a church in his honour. Two years later the saint's remains were moved into the new church in Assisi. It was called the Basilica of San Francesco. During the next hundred years or so, some of the most celebrated Italian artists decorated the walls and roof with wonderful paintings, called frescos, some of which showed the life of Saint Francis.

Sadly, in 1997, the famous church and many of the frescos were seriously damaged by earthquakes. Much of the nearby town of Foligno was destroyed, including the belltower, which is said to have stood by the very spot where Francis once sold some of his father's cloth and a horse.

After Francis died, the Order of the Friars Minor which he had begun was renamed the Franciscan Order. Today there are Franciscans in many countries throughout the world.

Saint Francis is remembered each year on 4th October.